Selected Poems

A. R. AMMONS

Selected Poems

A. R. AMMONS

Cornell University Press   ITHACA, NEW YORK

First published 1968

Library of Congress Catalog Card Number: 68–17302

PRINTED IN THE UNITED STATES OF AMERICA
BY THE SCIENCE PRESS, INC.
BOUND BY VAIL-BALLOU PRESS, INC.

for my wife Phyllis and son John

Acknowledgments

The poems in this volume, arranged in chronological order of composition (1951–1964), are selected from four books: *Ommateum* (Dorrance & Company, 1955), *Expressions of Sea Level* (Ohio State University Press, 1964), *Corsons Inlet* (Cornell University Press, 1965), and *Northfield Poems* (Cornell University Press, 1966). The book *Tape for the Turn of the Year* (Cornell University Press, 1965) is a single long poem, from which I have not attempted to make selections.

I would like to express my gratitude to the editors of the following publications for first publishing the poems listed:

Hudson Review: "I Went Out to the Sun," "The Whale-boat Struck," "Hymn," "The Watch," "Prospecting," "Silver," "Hardweed Path Going," "Bourn," "Guide," "Risks and Possibilities," "Terrain," "Bridge," "Unsaid," "Raft," "River," "Nelly Myers," "Motion for Motion," "Corsons Inlet," "Reflective," "Contingency," and "Interference."

Poetry: "Gravelly Run," "Joshua Tree," "Close-up," "Composing," "Mansion," "Expressions of Sea Level," "Halfway," "Landscape with Figures," "Dark Song," and "World."

Accent: "Whose Timeless Reach," "Driving Through," "Hymn II," "Hymn III," "Ritual for Eating the World," "Mountain Liar," "Thaw," "The Wind Coming Down From," and "The Golden Mean."

Epoch: "Coon Song," "Lines," "Dunes," "Moment," "Butterflyweed," and "Winter Scene." *The New York Times*: "Trap," "Loss," and "Recovery." *Quarterly Review of Literature*: "The Strait," "The Constant," and "Glass."

Discourse: "Prodigal" and "Jungle Knot." *Modern Occasions*: "Peak" and "Passage." *The Nation*: "Visit" and "Portrait." *Trojan Horse*: "Kind" and "Height."

Chelsea: "Motion." *Chicago Choice*: "Batsto." *Compass Review*: "The Wide Land." *Emerson Review*: "Still." *Impetus*: "Identity." *Partisan Review*: "March Song." *Shenandoah*: "The Yucca Moth." *Tri-Quarterly*: "Saliences."

The poems selected from *Expressions of Sea Level* are reprinted by permission of Ohio State University Press.

A. R. AMMONS

Rome, Italy
October 30, 1967

Contents

[x]

Selected Poems

A. R. AMMONS

So I Said I Am Ezra

So I said I am Ezra
and the wind whipped my throat
gaming for the sounds of my voice
      I listened to the wind
go over my head and up into the night
Turning to the sea I said
          I am Ezra
but there were no echoes from the waves
The words were swallowed up
     in the voice of the surf
or leaping over swells
lost themselves oceanward
        Over the bleached and broken fields
I moved my feet and turning from the wind
       that ripped sheets of sand
       from the beach and threw them
       like seamists across the dunes
swayed as if the wind were taking me away
and said
          I am Ezra
As a word too much repeated
falls out of being
so I Ezra went out into the night
like a drift of sand
and splashed among the windy oats
that clutch the dunes
of unremembered seas

The Sap Is Gone Out of the Trees

The sap is gone out of the trees
in the land of my birth
and the branches droop
    The rye is rusty in the fields
and the oatgrains are light in the wind
The combine sucks at the fields
    and coughs out dry mottled straw
The bags of grain are chaffy and light

The oatfields said Oh
and Oh said the wheatfields as the dusting
combine passed over
and long after the dust was gone
    Oh they said
and looked around at the stubble and straw
The sap is gone out of the hollow straws
and the marrow out of my bones
              They are
    brittle and dry
    and painful in this land

The wind whipped at my carcass saying
How shall I
    coming from these fields
water the fields of earth
    and I said Oh
    and fell down in the dust

I Went Out to the Sun

I went out to the sun
where it burned over a desert willow
and getting under the shade of the willow
I said
     It's very hot in this country
The sun said nothing so I said
      The moon has been talking about you
and he said
     Well what is it this time

     She says it's her own light
He threw his flames out so far
they almost scorched the top of the willow
     Well I said of course I don't know

The sun went on and the willow was glad
I found an arroyo and dug for water
which I got muddy and then clear
so I drank a lot
and washed the salt from my eyes
and taking off my shirt
hung it on the willow to dry and said
     This land where whirlwinds
walking at noon in tall columns of dust
     take stately turns about the desert
     is a very dry land
So I went to sleep under the willow tree

When the moon came up it was cold
and reaching to the willow for my shirt

I said to the moon
        You make it a pretty night
so she smiled

A night lizard rattled stems behind me
and the moon said
        I see over the mountain
        the sun is angry
Not able to see him I called and said
        Why are you angry with the moon
        since all at last must be lost
        to the great vacuity

The Whaleboat Struck

The whaleboat struck
and we came ashore
to the painted faces
    O primitives I said
and the arrow sang to my throat
Leaving myself on the shore
I went away
and when a heavy wind caught me I said
    My body lies south
    given over to vultures and flies
and wrung my hands
so the wind went on
Another day a wind came saying
    Bones
    lovely and white
    lie on the southern sand
    the ocean has washed bright
I said
    O bones in the sun
and went south
The flies were gone
The vultures no longer searched
the ends of my hingeless bones
for a trace of lean or gristle
Breathing the clean air
I picked up a rib
    to draw figures in the sand
till there is no roar in the ocean
no green in the sea

till the northwind flings no waves
across the open sea
I running in and out with the waves
I singing old Devonshire airs

Turning a Moment to Say So Long

Turning a moment to say so long
      to the spoken
      and seen
      I stepped into
the implicit pausing sometimes
on the way to listen to unsaid things
At a boundary of mind
      Oh I said brushing up
      against the unseen
      and whirling on my heel
      said
      I have overheard too much
Peeling off my being I plunged into
the well
The fingers of the water splashed
      to grasp me up
      but finding only
      a few shafts
of light
      too quick to grasp
      became hysterical
      jumped up and down
      and wept copiously
So I said I'm sorry dear well but
went on deeper
finding patched innertubes beer cans
and black roothairs along the way
but went on deeper

till darkness snuffed the shafts of light
against the well's side
night kissing
the last bubbles from my lips

Dying in a Mirthful Place

Dying in a mirthful place
I looked around at the dim lights
the hips and laughing throats
and the motions of the dance
and the wine the lovely wine
and turning to death said
    I thought you knew propriety
Death embarrassed stuttered
so I watched the lips
and hurried away to a hill in Arizona
where in the soil was such a noiseless
mirth and death
that I lay down and placed my head
    by a great boulder
The next morning I was dead
    excepting a few peripheral cells
and the buzzards
waiting for a savoring age to come
sat over me in mournful conversations
that sounded excellent to my eternal ear

With Ropes of Hemp

With ropes of hemp
I lashed my body to the great oak
saying odes for the fiber of the oakbark
and the oakwood saying supplications
to the root mesh
deep and reticular in the full earth
through the night saying these
and early into the wild unusual dawn
chanting hysterical though quiet
watching the ropes ravel
and the body go raw
    while eternity
greater than the ravelings of a rope
waited with me patient in my experiment
Oh I said listening to the raucous
words of the nightclouds
the soul is shadowy
fleet with the wildness of wings

Under the grip of my bonds
I say Oh and melt beyond the ruthless coil
but return again saying odes in the night
where I stand splintered to the oak
gathering the dissentient ghosts of my spirit
into the oakheart
I in the night standing saying oaksongs
entertaining my soul to me

Doxology

Heterodoxy with Ennui

Should I bold in a moment intrude
upon a silence, hold my hands properly,
crossed, in a mock eternity,
would someone use my lips
for an expiation?

I have heard the silent owl near death
sees wildly with the comprehension of fire;
have drunk from those eyes.

Transplanted my soul to the wind, wound
my days round the algae of rapid streams,
wedded my bones to the throat of flame,
spirited.

You have heard it said of old time
the streets shall flow blood, but the streets
swept out with the flood
shall be deposited upon sand.
You have this word for a fulfillment.

An unconstrained fluidity prevails, abides;
whole notes are rocks
and men *thirty-seconds*,
all in descending scales,
unvigiled bastardies of noise:
the motion of permanence.

Marble, pottery, signs endure,

support fluency, scrollwork;
where violins ornament, fingers,
offended with needles of care,
articulate poised domes.
This love for the thin and fleet
will race through the water-content
of my heavy death.

I die at the vernal equinox
and disorder like a kissing bug
quaffs my bonds: if I ascend,
I shall be congratulatory,
but if they fawn, desire
a season before immortality.

Detain me among the spiral designs
of an ancient amphora: fulfillment
comes before me like spiral designs
on an ancient amphora in which detain me,
fixed in rigid speed.

II

Orthodoxy with Achievement

Silent as light in dismal transit
through the void, I, evanescent,
sibilant among my parts,
fearing the eclipse of a possible glance
and not glancing, shut-eyed,
crouch froglike upon my brain,
hover and keep dark,
fervor opposed by dread,
activity numbed by its mixed result,
till some awaited drop falls
upon the mound and chaos

perfects the eternity of my silence.

I cannot count the forms,
thrown upon the wheel, delineated,
that have risen and returned
without accretion; but the spirit
drops falling upon wings
and preens the day with its call:
none say where in the silence it sleeps.

Though the sound of my voice
is a firmamental flaw, my self, in the rockheart,
in southern oakmoss blown tangled,
its supple pincers snaring
new forks of life, braiding thin limbs
of the wateroak on gooseberry hills
beside swamps where the raccoon runs
and dips his paw in the run-of-the-swamp
musky branchwater for darting crawfish
scuttling a mudwake before them; my self,
voluble in the dark side of hills
and placid bays, while the sun grows
increasing atmosphere to the sea,
correcting the fault of dawn; my self,
the drought of unforested plains,
the trilobite's voice,
the loquacity of an alien room troubled
by a blowfly, requires my entertainment
while we learn the vowels of silence.

III

Paradox with Variety

The temple stands in a rainforest
where bones have a quick ending.

Ephemeral as wings in fire

transparent leaves droop in the earth-steam;
growth and decay swallow the traces
of recent paths.

I went in. On one side sat the god of creation; on the other,
the god of destruction. Hatred held their eyes. Going deeper
to the next chamber, I found the god of destruction and the
god of creation tangled sensually on the floor; they gnawed
and procreated. In the next chamber was majesty: one god
sat staring at his golden walls.

I hear an organ playing through the morning rain;
it sounds like the memory of quilting women.
Between the organ and me, California poppies furl
like splotches of conceit
in the light and silent rain.
A robin peeks up from the grass
and rattles a ladybug in his beak.
Mr. Farnham says
life is fearfully complex.

When I was lustful I drew twenty maidens
from the Well of Sacrifice
and took them to Cozumel.
The priests of the steep temples
longed to smear my body
with blue ointment.
We've all died since
and all has been forgotten.
Strangers drop pebbles
into the Hole of Water:
it is too still.

Should I mistake khaki blood on foreign snow
for cherry ices, my mind would freeze;
but Red blood is interesting:

[14]

its vessels on the snow
are museums of eternity.

When stone and drought meet in high places,
the hand instructed by thirst
chips grace into solidity and Hellas
like a broken grape upon marmoreal locks
clarifies eternity. Had I come in the season
when sheep nibble windy grasses,
I would have gone out of the earth
listening for grasses
and the stippling feet of sheep
on sinking rocks.

I like to walk down windowless corridors
and, going with the draft,
feel the boost of perpendicularity,
directional and rigid;
concision of the seraphim,
artificial lighting.

Sometimes the price of my content
consumes its purchase
and martyrs' cries, echoing my peace,
rise sinuously like smoke
out of my ashen soul.

Having Been Interstellar

Having been interstellar
    and in the treble clef

by great expense of
        climbing mountains
        lighting crucible fires
in the catacombs

        among the hunted
and the trapped in tiers
        seeking the distillate
        answering direct
the draft of earthless air

he turned in himself
        helplessly as in sleep

and went out into the growth of rains
        and when the rains
        taking him
had gone away in spring

        no one knew
that he had ever flown
        he was no less
        no more known
to stones he left a stone

Coming to Sumer

Coming to Sumer and the tamarisks on the river
I Ezra with unsettling love
rifled the mud and wattle huts
for recent mournings
with gold leaves
and lapis lazuli beads
in the neat braids loosening from the skull
    Looking through the wattles to the sun
I said
It has rained some here in this place
unless snow falls heavily in the hills
to do this
    The floor was smooth with silt
and river weeds hanging gray
on the bent reeds spoke saying
Everything is even here as you can see
    Firing the huts
I abandoned the unprofitable poor
unequal even in the bone
    to disrespect
    and casual with certainty
watched an eagle wing as I went
to king and priest

I Struck a Diminished Seventh

I struck a diminished seventh
and sat down
to wait
     for the universal word
Come word
I said
azalea word
gel precipitate
while I
     the primitive spindle
binding the poles of earth and air
give you
with river ease
a superior appreciation
equaling winged belief
     It had almost come
I perishing for deity stood up
drying my feet
when the minor challenge was ignored
and death came over sieving me

When I Set Fire to the Reed Patch

When I set fire to the reed patch
that autumn evening
the wind whipped volleys of shot
from the bursting joints
and armies bristling defensive interest
rushed up over the fringing hills
and stared into the fire

I laughed my self to death
and they
legs afire
eyelashes singed
swept in flooding up the lovely
expressions of popping light
and hissing thorns of flame

Clashing midfire
the armies quite unwound
the intentions of the fire
and snuffed the black reeds smoking out
but like destroyed mountains
left deposits
that will insure
deep mulch for next year's shoots
the greenest hope
autumn ever
left this patch of reeds

A Treeful of Cleavage Flared Branching

A treeful of cleavage flared branching
through my flesh and cagey
I sat down mid-desert
and heaping hugged up between my knees
an altarcone from the sand
and addressed it with water dreams

The wind
chantless of rain in the open place
spun a sifting hum
in slow circles round my sphere of grief
and the sun
inched countless arms
under the periphery of my disc of sight
eager for the golden thing

There must be time I said
to dream these dreams real
and the sun
startled by the sound of time
said Oh
and whirling in his arms
ran off across the sky
Heaping the sand
sharpening the cone of my god I said
I have oracles to seek

Drop leaf shade
the wet cuticle of the leaf tipped in shade
yielded belief

[20]

to the fixed will and there
where the wind like wisdom
sweeps clean the lust prints of the sun
lie my bones entombed
with the dull mound of my god
in bliss

I Set It My Task

I set it my task
to gather the stones of earth
    into one place
the water modeled sand molded stones
   from
     the water images
     of riverbeds in drought
    from the boundaries of mind
    from
      sloping farms
      and altitudes of ice and
to mount upon the highest stone
a cardinal
chilled in the attitude of song

But the wind has sown loose dreams
in my eyes
    and telling unknown tongues
drawn me out beyond the land's end
    and rising in long
    parabolas of bliss
borne me safety
from all those ungathered stones

A Crippled Angel

A crippled angel bent in a scythe of grief
mourned in an empty lot
    Passing by I stopped
amused that immortality should grieve
and said
It must be exquisite

Smoke came out of the angel's ears
       the axles
    of slow handwheels of grief
and under the white lids of its eyes
bulged tears of purple light
Watching the agony diffuse in
      shapeless loss
I interposed a harp
    The atmosphere possessed it eagerly
and the angel
saying prayers for the things of time

let its fingers drop and burn
the lyric strings provoking wonder

Grief sounded like an ocean rose
      in bright clothes
and the fire
breaking out on the limbs rising
caught up the branching wings
    in a flurry of ascent
Taking a bow I shot transfixing
the angel midair

all miracle hanging fire
on rafters of the sky

I Came upon a Plateau

I came upon a plateau
where mesquite roots
crazed the stone
    and rains
moved glinting dust
down the crevices
    Calling off rings
        to a council of peaks
I said
Spare me man's redundancy
and putting on bright clothes
sat down in the flat orthodoxy

Quivering with courtesy
a snake drew thrust in sines
and circles from his length
rearing coils of warning white
    Succumbing in the still ecstasy
sinuous through white rows of scales
I caved in upon eternity
saying This use is colorless

A pious person his heart
looted and burnt
    sat under a foundation
a windy cloak clutched round his bones
and said
When the razed temple cooled
I went in
and gathered these

relics of holy urns
Behold beneath this cloak
          and I looked in
at the dark whirls of dust

The peaks coughing bouldered
laughter shook to pieces
and the snake shed himself in ripples
across a lake of sand

Whose Timeless Reach

I Ezra the dying
portage of these deathless thoughts
stood on a hill in
the presence of the mountain
and said wisdom is
too wise for man it
is for gods and gods have little
use for it so I do not know what
to do with it
and animals use it only when
    their teeth start to fall and it
is too late to do anything
else but *be* wise and stay
out of the way
The eternal will not lie
down on any temporal hill
    The frozen mountain rose and broke
its tireless lecture of repose
and said death does
not take away it
ends giving halts bounty and
    Bounty I said thinking of ships
that I might take and helm right
out through space
dwarfing these safe harbors and
their values
taking the Way in whose timeless reach
cool thought unpunishable
by bones eternally glides

Driving Through

In the desert midnight I said
taking out my notebook I
   am astonished
though widely traveled having
seen Empire State and Palestine, Texas
and San Miguel de Allende
to mention extremes
and sharpened my pencil on the sole
   of my shoe

The mountains running skidded
over the icy mirages of the moon
and fell down tumbling
   laughing for breath
on the cool dunes
The stone mosaics of the flattest
places (parting lake-gifts) grouped
   in colors and
played games at imagery: a green
tiger with orange eyes, an Orpheus
with moving fingers
   Fontal the shrubs flooded
everything with cool
water

I sat down against a brimming smoketree
to watch and morning found the
desert reserved
trembling at its hot and rainless task

Driving through
you would never suspect
the midnight rite or seeing my lonely house
guess it will someday hold
laurel and a friend

Song

Merging into place against a slope of trees,
I extended my arms and
took up the silence and spare leafage.
I lost my head first, the cervical meat
clumping off in rot,
baring the spinal heart to wind and ice

which work fast.
The environment lost no self-possession.
In spring, termites with tickling feet
aereated my veins.
A gall-nesting wren took my breath

flicking her wings, and
far into summer the termites found the heart.
No sign now shows the place,
all these seasons since,
but a hump of sod below the leaves
where chipmunks dig.

Hymn

I know if I find you I will have to leave the earth
and go on out
    over the sea marshes and the brant in bays
and over the hills of tall hickory
and over the crater lakes and canyons
and on up through the spheres of diminishing air
past the blackset noctilucent clouds
      where one wants to stop and look
way past all the light diffusions and bombardments
up farther than the loss of sight
    into the unseasonal undifferentiated empty stark

And I know if I find you I will have to stay with the earth
inspecting with thin tools and ground eyes
trusting the microvilli sporangia and simplest
    coelenterates
and praying for a nerve cell
with all the soul of my chemical reactions
and going right on down where the eye sees only traces

You are everywhere partial and entire
You are on the inside of everything and on the outside

I walk down the path down the hill where the sweetgum
has begun to ooze spring sap at the cut
and I see how the bark cracks and winds like no other bark
chasmal to my ant-soul running up and down
and if I find you I must go out deep into your
    far resolutions
and if I find you I must stay here with the separate leaves

Hymn II

So when the year had come full round
I rose
and went out to the naked mountain
to see
the single peachflower on the sprout

blooming through a side of ribs
    possibly a colt's
and I endured each petal separately
and moved in orisons with the sepals

I lay
    said the sprouting stump
in the path of Liberty

Tyranny though I said is very terrible
and sat down leeward of the blossom
    to be blessed
and was startled by
a lost circling bee

The large sun setting red I went
down to the stream
    and wading in
let your cold water run over my feet

Hymn III

In the hour of extreme

    importance

when clots thicken
in outlying limbs and
    warmth retreats

to mourn
the thinning garrison of pulse

keep my tongue loose
to sing possible

    changes

that might redeem

might in iron phrases
    clang the skies

bells and my jangling eyes
ringing you in
    to claim me

shriven celebrant
your love's new-reasoned singer

    home

dead on arrival

The Watch

When the sun went down and the night came on
coming over the fields and up the driveway
to the rose arbor and the backporch posts

I gathered myself together from dispersing dark
and went up into the mountains
and sitting down on the round rock beyond the trees

kindled my thoughts
blowing the coals of my day's bright conscious
and said

all across the plains my voice going silently and down
among the stumps where the swamp cuts through
and in between among the villages of hill country

Now close your eyes
Sleep
Shut out the world from the dark sweet freshening
    of your quiet hearts
Lie loose in the deep waters
Do not be afraid to
give yourselves up to drowning in undefended rest

If a dust storm blows up out of the west I will run
down the mountain and go through all the homes
and wake you up

If a new fire appears in the sky I will let you know
in time

so you can know it should it claim you

I will have all your beings in mind burning like a watchfire
and when the night has grown thin and weak
and the full coyotes have given up their calls

I will move up close to the eternal and
saying nine praises
commend you to it and to the coming sun

March Song

At a bend in the stream by willows
I paused to be with the cattails
   their long flat leaves
and tall stems
bleached by wind and winter light

and winter had kept them
   edged down into the quiet eddy of the bend
tight with ice

O willows I said how you return
gold to the nakedness of your limbs
   coming again out of that country
into the longer sun

and Oh I said turning to the fluffy cattails
loosened to the approaching winds of spring
what a winter you leave in the pale stems
   of your becoming

Ritual for Eating the World

At a bend in the rocks there hung
inexplicably a rope
and musing I said
When I die don't bury me
under no weeping willer tree

It's I thought a hangman's loop
provided by my warmer ghoul to
raise me out of care

or god's own private fishing hook
for glaring people
who sit wasted in the sun
on rocks

But put me up in a high dry place
unavailable to the coyote's face

It's what I said old mountain
climbers left
dangling

The wind rides blade on mesa tops

Oh when I die don't bury me
under no weeping willer tree

and there being besides old bush
and distance nothing but a rope
I engaged myself with it but

it broke
and all through the heaving night

making day I faced

piecemeal the sordid
reacceptance of my world

The Wide Land

Having split up the chaparral
blasting my sight
the wind said
   You know I'm
      the result of
forces beyond my control
I don't hold it against you
I said
It's all right I understand

Those pressure bowls and cones
the wind said
are giants in their continental gaits
I know I said I know
they're blind giants
Actually the wind said I'm
   if anything beneficial
    resolving extremes
filling up lows with highs
No I said you don't have
to explain
It's just the way things are

Blind in the wide land I
turned and risked my feet
to loose stones and sudden

alterations of height

Batsto

After two gray sunless days of warm
noreaster windy rains the sun breaking
clear this morning, over the bayside
field the sparrowhawk foraging in the
oval air, we took Route 9 north through
Pleasantville, past the pleasant
inviting cemetery crisp with light,
over the railroad, crosstown to the
Absecon meadows and into the sycamore
leaf-letting hills beyond and through
the housing development with groves
of old leaf-keeping darker oaks and

northward past Seaview Country Club
with the high round dining room and
young rich men in casuals crossing the
street to the golf-links and on past
fields and hedges, the scarlotry of
maple leaves, sassafras and skinny
birch resplendent in the clean sun,
the winding flat highway, empty
but for slight local traffic, and onto
Garden State Parkway to bridge the
wide-mouthed Mullica River that spreads
out in brown still meadows to the sea,
an occasional gull, the skeletal
cedar upriver against the land, off
to secondary roads not too well marked
and along the north bank of the

Mullica westward into the Wharton
Tract, now a state park, with ghost
towns and endless acres in neglect,

stopping at a pinerise to see the
cemetery of the French family, death
after more than a century light as
the morning sun, where Thomas French,
a year older than his wife, lies since
1844, his wife three years later
giving up her heavy grief, lying
down beside him, their secret union
invisible in the green needles of
the great pine that branches now
into their rest, looking where Levi
Scott, four years old in 1800, went
down beneath his thin tall slab, may
the child keep innocent of treason, and

on to Crowley Landing on the left
between river and road, now a campsite
and picnic ground, where we took
pictures, wild mullein starring the
grounds, a yucca group with dead
flower-spears off in a clearing, in
the center a mound of old chimney
bricks with wasp dust and gold grasses
and a yard tree, broken off, with
slender sprouts nude, swamp cedar
standing around in clumps like persons
edging the openings, by the river now
narrower twists of white birch
thin-twigged and leafless, and

around two curves to Batsto, the
tower of the mansion house first seen,

like the towers of shore women gazing
the sea's return, a confluence of
roads and streams, the bog-iron works
and Revolutionary cannon balls, iron
hearths and iron oxen-shoes, seeing
a nail made and headed from nail rod,
the company store, and men from
Trenton writing the place up for the
Sunday paper, wasps drunk with fall
warmth, a beautiful November noon by
the grist mill and the meal-honed
wood, the carriage house and small
seats, the sty with the iron-bowled
furnace for scalding, on the third
floor of the mansion a strict stairway
to the slaves' underground railroad,
and

weakening to the presence of a foreign
past and to the keeping of old things,
back home by Route 30 and the White
Horse Pike, by the farmers' stands,
Naval Air Base and to the sea's edge.

Mountain Liar

The mountains said they were
       tired of lying down
and wanted to know what
       I could do about
getting them off the ground

Well close your eyes I said
       and I'll see if I can
by seeing into your nature
       tell where you've been wronged
What do you think you want to do
       They said Oh fly

My hands are old
       and crippled keep no lyre
but if that is your true desire
       and conforms roughly
with your nature I said
       I don't see why
we shouldn't try
       to see something along that line

Hurry they said and snapped shut
       with rocky sounds their eyes
I closed mine and sure enough
       the whole range flew
gliding on interstellar ice

They shrieked with joy and peeked
       as if to see below
but saw me as before there

foolish without my lyre
We haven't budged they said
You wood

Gravelly Run

I don't know somehow it seems sufficient
to see and hear whatever coming and going is,
losing the self to the victory
    of stones and trees,
of bending sandpit lakes, crescent
round groves of dwarf pine:

for it is not so much to know the self
as to know it as it is known
    by galaxy and cedar cone,
as if birth had never found it
and death could never end it:

the swamp's slow water comes
down Gravelly Run fanning the long
    stone-held algal
hair and narrowing roils between
the shoulders of the highway bridge:

holly grows on the banks in the woods there,
and the cedars' gothic-clustered
    spires could make
green religion in winter bones:

so I look and reflect, but the air's glass
jail seals each thing in its entity:

no use to make any philosophies here:
    I see no
god in the holly, hear no song from
the snowbroken weeds: Hegel is not the winter

yellow in the pines: the sunlight has never
heard of trees: surrendered self among
    unwelcoming forms: stranger,
hoist your burdens, get on down the road.

Prospecting

Coming to cottonwoods, an
orange rockshelf,
and in the gully
an edging of stream willows,

I made camp
and turned my mule loose
to graze in the dark
evening of the mountain.

Drowsed over the coals
and my loneliness
like an inner image went
out and shook
hands with the willows,

and running up the black scarp
tugged the heavy moon
up and over into light,

and on a hill-thorn of sage
called with the coyotes
and told ghost stories to
a night circle of lizards.
Tipping on its handle
the Dipper unobtrusively
poured out the night.

At dawn returning, wet
to the hips with meetings,
my loneliness woke me up

and we merged refreshed into
the breaking of camp and day.

Joshua Tree

The wind
rounding the gap
found me there
weeping under a
Joshua Tree
and Oh I said
I am mortal all right
and cannot live,
by roads
stopping to wait
for no one coming,
moving on
to dust
and burned weeds,
having no liturgy,
no pilgrim
from my throat
singing news of joy,
no dome, alabaster wall,
no eternal city:
the wind said
Wayfaring and wandering
is not for mortals
who should raise
the cock
that cries their
dawns in and
cannot always be coming to
unbroken country:

settle here
by this Joshua Tree
and make a well:
unlike wind
that dies and
never dies I said
I must go on
consigned to
form that will not
let me loose
except to death
till some
syllable's rain
anoints my tongue
and makes it sing
to strangers:
if it does not rain
find me wasted by roads:
enter angling through
my cage
and let my ribs
sing me out.

Thaw

Winter over, ice-bound
mind better not
rush to a spring-meet fast;
might trip, stiff thoughts,
    shatter:
better not warm up too
close to sun;
might melt, run, gullies
caking off the good
firm country of the brain.

Better go slow,
bend with the gradual movement,
let sap flow but
keep an eye on any
thermal swell rising at
    glassy mind.

If it gets loose wind
will take it
riddling through the underbrush,
but if it stays
solid brilliant ice
tulip root
    warm in coming
will splinter it.

The Wind Coming Down From

summit and blue air
said I am sorry for you
and lifting past
said you
are mere dust which I
as you see control

yet nevertheless are
instrument of miracle

and rose
out of earshot but
returning in a slow loop
said while
I am always just this bunch of
compensating laws
pushed, pushing
not air or motion
but the motion of air

I coughed
and the wind said
Ezra will live
to see your last
sun come up again

I turned (as I will) to weeds and
the wind went off
carving
monuments through a field of stone
monuments whose shape

wind cannot arrest but
taking hold on
changes

while Ezra
   listens from terraces of mind
wind cannot reach or
weedroots of my low-feeding shiver

Silver

        I thought Silver must have snaked logs
        when young:
she couldn't stand to have the line brush her lower hind leg:
in blinded halter she couldn't tell what had loosened behind her
           and was coming
as downhill
to rush into her crippling her to the ground:

and when she almost went to sleep, me dreaming at the slow plow,
I would
at dream's end turning over the mind to a new chapter
        let the line drop and touch her leg
        and she would
bring the plow out of the ground with speed but wisely
fall soon again into the slow requirements of our dreams:
how we turned at the ends of rows without sense to new furrows
and went back
        flicked by
        cornblades and hearing the circling in
the cornblades of horseflies in pursuit:

        I hitch up early, the raw spot on Silver's shoulder
sore to the collar,
get a wrench and change the plow's bull-tongue for a sweep,
and go out, wrench in my hip pocket for later adjustments,
        down the ditch-path
by the white-bloomed briars, wet crabgrass, cattails,
        and rusting ferns,
riding the plow handles down,
   keeping the sweep's point from the ground,

[54]

the smooth bar under the plow gliding,
the traces loose, the raw spot wearing its soreness out
in the gentle movement to the fields:

when snake-bitten in the spring pasture grass
Silver came up to the gate and stood head-down enchanted
in her fate
I found her sorrowful eyes by accident and knew:
nevertheless the doctor could not keep her from all
the consequences, rolls in the sand, the blank extension
of limbs,
head thrown back in the dust,
useless unfocusing eyes, belly swollen
wide as I was tall
and I went out in the night and saw her in the solitude
of her wildness:

but she lived and one day half got up
and looking round at the sober world took me back
into her eyes
and then got up and walked and plowed again;
mornings her swollen snake-bitten leg wept bright as dew
and dried to streaks of salt leaked white from the hair.

Hardweed Path Going

>   Every evening, down into the hardweed
going,
the slop bucket heavy, held-out, wire handle
freezing in the hand, put it down a minute, the jerky
smooth unspilling levelness of the knees,
>   meditation of a bucket rim,
lest the wheat meal,
floating on clear greasewater, spill,
down the grown-up path:

>>   don't forget to slop the hogs,
>>   feed the chickens,
>>   water the mule,
>>   cut the kindling,
>>   build the fire,
>>   call up the cow:

>   supper is over, it's starting to get
dark early,
better get the scraps together, mix a little meal in,
nothing but swill.

>   The dead-purple woods hover on the west.
I know those woods.
Under the tall, ceiling-solid pines, beyond the edge of
field and brush, where the wild myrtle grows,
>   I let my jo-reet loose.
A jo-reet is a bird. Nine weeks of summer he
sat on the well bench in a screened box,
a stick inside to walk on,
>   "jo-reet," he said, "jo-reet."

and I
would come up to the well and draw the bucket down
deep into the cold place where red and white marbled
clay oozed the purest water, water celebrated
throughout the county:
>"Grits all gone?"
>"jo-reet."

Throw a dipper of cold water on him. Reddish-black
flutter.
>"reet, reet, reet!"

>Better turn him loose before
cold weather comes on.
>Doom caving in
>inside
>any pleasure, pure
>attachment
>of love.

Beyond the wild myrtle away from cats I turned him loose
and his eye asked me what to do, where to go;
he hopped around, scratched a little, but looked up at me.
Don't look at me. Winter is coming.
Disappear in the bushes. I'm tired of you and will
be alone hereafter. I will go dry in my well.
>I will turn still.

Go south. Grits is not available in any natural form.
Look under leaves, try mushy logs, the floors of pinywoods.
South into the dominion of bugs.

>They're good woods.

But lay me out if a mourning dove far off in the dusky pines
>starts.

>Down the hardweed path going,
leaning, balancing, away from the bucket, to
Sparkle, my favorite hog, sparse, fine black hair,

grunted while feeding if rubbed,
scratched against the hair, or if talked to gently:
got the bottom of the slop bucket:
        "Sparkle
        "You hungry?
        "Hungry, girly?"
blowing, bubbling in the trough.

        Waiting for the first freeze:
"Think it's going to freeze tonight?" say the neighbors,
the neighbors, going by.

        Hog-killing.

Sparkle, when the axe tomorrow morning falls
and the rush is made to open your throat,
I will sing, watching dry-eyed as a man, sing my
        love for you in the tender feedings.

        She's nothing but a hog, boy.

Bleed out, Sparkle, the moon-chilled bleaches
        of your body hanging upside-down
hardening through the mind and night of the first freeze.

Close-up

Are all these stones
         yours
I said
and the mountain
pleased

but reluctant to
admit my praise could move it much

shook a little
and rained a windrow ring of stones
to show
that it was so

Stonefelled I got
up addled with dust

and shook
         myself
without much consequence

Obviously I said it doesn't pay
to get too
close up to
         greatness

and the mountain friendless wept
         and said
it couldn't help
itself

Bourn

When I got past relevance
the singing shores
told me to turn back

but I took the outward gray
to be
some meaning of foreign light

trying to get through and
when I looked back saw
the shores were dancing

willows of grief and
from willows it was not far to
look back on waves

So I came to
the decimal of being,
entered and was gone

What light there
no tongue turns to tell
to willow and calling shore

though willows weep and shores sing always

Composing

An orchestration of events,
memories,
intellections, wounds,
hard throats:
a clustering of years into phrases,
motifs, a

keying to somber D-flat
or brilliant A:
an emergence
of minor meanings,
the loft of flutes, oboes, bassoons:
percussion,
the critical cymbal

crashing grief out
or like a peacock's tail
unfolding into spirit:
the derelict breakage of days, weeks,
hours, reorganizing,
orienting to the riding movement,

hawklike,
but keener in wings,
in shadow deeper:
a swerving into the underside
gathering
dream images,
the hidden flight of red-black cries,

darkness,

the ghosts re-rising,
the eyeless, furious,
mangled ones:
then two motions like cliffs
opposing, the orchestration at
first

too torn, but going back
finding new lights to doom
dark resurrections
till the large curve of meaning
stands apart
like a moon cusp or horn
singing with a higher soundless sound.

Orientale

The pebble spoke and down
came the sun
    its plume
brushing through space as

over smooth sea-reaching stream
bent reed
    lets sodden leaf
arrow-ripples cut

and acorn husk wind-whirled
ran out and caught the sun
    in its burred cup
and said Look

to everyone standing on
edge of fern leaf watching
    the other edge
become imaginary as

waterbirds low-flying through
islands snake-long dark offshore
    Acorn husk got
no attention and even

the universe could sundering
hold no ear
    What somebody asked did
the pebble say

and sea colander washed
aland said Nothing

nothing exists
and everybody watched to
see if fern leaf could
reappear with its lost edge
and when
snow fell went in

Mansion

So it came time
    for me to cede myself
and I chose
the wind
    to be delivered to

The wind was glad
    and said it needed all
the body
it could get
    to show its motions with

and wanted to know
    willingly as I hoped it would
if it could do
something in return
    to show its gratitude

When the tree of my bones
    rises from the skin I said
come and whirlwinding
stroll my dust
    around the plain

so I can see
    how the ocotillo does
and how saguaro-wren is
and when you fall
    with evening

fall with me here

where we can watch
the closing up of day
and think how morning breaks

Prodigal

After the shifts and dis-
continuities, after the congregations of orders,
    black masses floating through
    mind's boreal clarity, icebergs in fog,
flotillas of wintering ducks weathering the night,
    chains of orders, multifilamentous chains
    knobbed with possibility, disoriented
chains, winding back on themselves, unwinding,
    intervolving, spinning, breaking off

    (nomads clustering at dusk into tents of sleep,
disorganizing, widening out again with morning)
    after the mental

    blaze and gleam,
the mind in both motions building and tearing down,
    running to link effective chains, ·
    establish molecules of meaning,
frameworks, to
    perfect modes of structuring
    (so days can bend to trellising
and pruned take shape,
    bloom into necessary event)

    after these motions, these vectors,
orders moving in and out of orders, collisions
    of orders, dispersions, the grasp weakens,

    the mind whirls, short of the unifying
reach, short of the heat
    to carry that forging:

after the visions of these losses, the spent
seer, delivered to wastage, risen
into ribs, consigns knowledge to
approximation, order to the vehicle
of change, and fumbles blind in blunt innocence
toward divine, terrible love.

Mechanism

Honor a going thing, goldfinch, corporation, tree,
        morality: any working order,
     animate or inanimate: it

has managed directed balance,
        the incoming and outgoing energies are working right,
     some energy left to the mechanism,

some ash, enough energy held
        to maintain the order in repair,
     assure further consumption of entropy,

expending energy to strengthen order:
        honor the persisting reactor,
     the container of change, the moderator: the yellow

bird flashes black wing-bars
        in the new-leaving wild cherry bushes by the bay,
     startles the hawk with beauty,

flitting to a branch where
        flash vanishes into stillness,
     hawk addled by the sudden loss of sight:

honor the chemistries, platelets, hemoglobin kinetics,
        the light-sensitive iris, the enzymic intricacies
     of control,

the gastric transformations, seed
        dissolved to acrid liquors, synthesized into
     chirp, vitreous humor, knowledge,

blood compulsion, instinct: honor the
          unique genes,
          molecules that reproduce themselves, divide into

sets, the nucleic grain transmitted
          in slow change through ages of rising and falling form,
          some cells set aside for the special work, mind

or perception rising into orders of courtship,
          territorial rights, mind rising
          from the physical chemistries

to guarantee that genes will be exchanged, male
          and female met, the satisfactions cloaking a deeper
          racial satisfaction:

heat kept by a feathered skin:
          the living alembic, body heat maintained (Bunsen
          burner under the flask)

so the chemistries can proceed, reaction rates
          interdependent, self-adjusting, with optimum
          efficiency—the vessel firm, the flame

staying: isolated, contained reactions! the precise and
          necessary worked out of random, reproducible,
          the handiwork redeemed from chance, while the

goldfinch, unconscious of the billion operations
          that stay its form, flashes, chirping (not a
          great songster) in the bay cherry bushes wild of leaf.

Guide

You cannot come to unity and remain material:
in that perception is no perceiver:
when you arrive
you have gone too far:
at the Source you are in the mouth of Death:

you cannot
turn around in
the Absolute: there are no entrances or exits
no precipitations of forms
to use like tongs against the formless:
no freedom to choose:

to be
you have to stop not-being and break
off from *is* to *flowing* and
this is the sin you weep and praise:
origin is your original sin:
the return you long for will ease your guilt
and you will have your longing:

the wind that is my guide said this: it
should know having
given up everything to eternal being but
direction:

how I said can I be glad and sad: but a man goes
from one foot to the other:
wisdom wisdom:
to be glad and sad at once is also unity
and death:

wisdom wisdom: a peachblossom blooms on a particular
tree on a particular day:
   unity cannot do anything in particular:

are these the thoughts you want me to think I said but
  the wind was gone and there was no more knowledge then.

The Golden Mean

What does
wisdom say:
wisdom says
do not put too much stress
on doing; sit some and wait,
if you can get
that self-contained:
but do not sit too much;
being can wear thin
without experience:
not too much stress on thrift
at the expense of living;
immaterial things like
life must be conserved against
materiality: however,
spending every dime you make
can exhaust all boundaries,
destroy resources and
recovery's means:
not too much stress on knowledge;
understanding, too, is a
high faculty
that should bear pleasurably on facts;
ordering, aligning,
comparing,
as processes, become diffuse in too
much massiveness:
but the acquisition
of thinking stuff is crucial

to knowledge
and to understanding:
wisdom says
do not love exceedingly:
you must withhold
enough to weather loss;
however, love thoroughly
and with the body
so women will respect and fear the little
man: though dainty
they will scoff
when not profoundly had: not too much
mind over body or
body over mind;
they are united in this life and should
blend to dual good or ill:
and do not stress
wisdom too much: if you lean neither
way, the golden
mean narrows
and rather than a way becomes a wire,
or altogether
vanishes, a
hypothetical line from which extremes
perpendicularly begin:
and if you do not
violate wisdom to some extent,
committing yourself fully,
without reserve,
and foolishly, you will not become *one*,
capable of direction,
selected to a single aim,
and you will be notable for nothing:

[74]

nothing in excess is
excessive nothingness:
go: but wisdom says do not go too far.

Risks and Possibilities

Here are some pretty things picked for you:

1)   dry thunder
rustling like water
down the sky's eaves

        is summer locust
in dogfennel weed

2)   the fieldwild
yellow daisy
        focusing dawn
inaugurates
the cosmos

3)   the universe comes
        to bear
on a willow-slip and
you cannot unwind
        a pebble
from its constellations

4)   chill frog-gibber
from grass
        or loose stone
is

        crucial as fieldwild
yellow daisy:

such propositions:
each thing boundless in its effect,

eternal in the working out
of its effect: each brush
of beetle-bristle against a twig
    and the whole
shifts, compensates, realigns:
the crawl of a slug
    on the sea's floor
quivers the moon to a new dimension:
bright philosophy,
    shake us all! here on the
bottom of an ocean of space
we babble words recorded
    in waves
of sound that
cannot fully disappear,
    washing up
like fossils on the shores of unknown worlds:

    nevertheless, taking our identities,
    we accept destruction:

    a tree, committed as a tree,
    cannot in a flood
        turn fish,
    sprout gills (leaves are
    a tree's gills) and fins:
        the molluscs
    dug out of mountain peaks
    are all dead:

oh I will be addled and easy and move
over this prairie in the wind's keep,
long-lying sierras blue-low in the distance:
I will glide and say little
(what would you have me say? I know nothing;

still, I cannot help singing)
and after much grace
I will pause
and break cactus water to your lips:

identity's strict confinement! a risk
    and possibility,
granted by mercy:
in your death is the mercy of your granted life:
    do not quibble:

    dry thunder in the locust weed!
    the supple willow-slip leafless in winter!
    the chill gibber of the frog
    stilled in nightsnake's foraging thrust!
    how ridiculous!
grim:
    enchanting:

repeating mid night these songs for these divisions

Terrain

The soul is a region without definite boundaries:
    it is not certain a prairie
can exhaust it
        or a range enclose it:
it floats (self-adjusting) like the continental mass,
    where it towers most
extending its deepest mantling base
        (exactly proportional):
does not flow all one way: there is a divide:
    river systems thrown like winter tree-shadows
against the hills: branches, runs, high lakes:
        stagnant lily-marshes:

is variable, has weather: floods unbalancing
    gut it, silt altering the
distribution of weight, the nature of content:
        whirlwinds move through it
or stand spinning like separate orders: the moon comes:
    there are barren spots: bogs, rising
by self-accretion from themselves, a growth into
        destruction of growth,
change of character,
    invasion of peat by poplar and oak: semiprecious
stones and precious metals drop from muddy water into mud:

it is an area of poise, really, held from tipping,
    dark wild water, fierce eels, countercurrents:
a habitat, precise ecology of forms
        mutually to some extent
tolerable, not entirely self-destroying: a crust afloat:

[79]

a scum, foam to the deep and other-natured:
but deeper than depth, too: a vacancy and swirl:

it may be spherical, light and knowledge merely
the iris and opening
to the dark methods of its sight: how it comes and
goes, ruptures and heals,
whirls and stands still: the moon comes: terrain.

Bridge

A tea garden shows you how:

      you sit in rhododendron shade
at table
on a pavilion-like lawn

      the sun midafternoon through the blooms
and you

watch lovers and single people
go over the steep moonbridge at the pond's narrows

where flies nip circles

      in the glass
and vanish in the widening sight except for an uncertain

      gauze memory of wings

and as you sip from the small thick cup
      held bird-warm
      in the hands

      you watch
the people
rising on the bridge

descend into the pond,
      where bridge and mirrorbridge merge

      at the bank
returning their images to themselves:
      a grove

of pepper trees (sgraffito)
        screens them into isolations of love or loneliness:

it is enough from this to think in the green tea scent
and turn to farther things:

when the spirit comes to the bridge of consciousness
and climbs higher and higher
        toward the peak no one reaches live
but where ascension
        and descension meet
completing the idea of a bridge

think where the body is,
        that going too deep

it may lose touch,
        wander a ghost in hell
        sing irretrievably in gloom,
and think

how the spirit silvery with vision may
break loose in high wind

        and go off weightless

body never to rise or spirit fall again to unity,
to lovers strolling through pepper-tree shade:

        paradise was when

Dante
regathered from height and depth
        came out onto the soft, green, level earth

into the natural light, come, sweat, bloodblessings,
        and thinning sheaf of days.

Coon Song

I got one good look
    in the raccoon's eyes
        when he fell from the tree
came to his feet
    and perfectly still
        seized the baying hounds
in his dull fierce stare,
    in that recognition all
        decision lost,
choice irrelevant, before the
    battle fell
        and the unwinding
of his little knot of time began:

        Dostoevsky would think
it important if the coon
    could choose to
        be back up the tree:
or if he could choose to be
    wagging by a swamp pond,
        dabbling at scuttling
crawdads: the coon may have
    dreamed in fact of curling
        into the holed-out gall
of a fallen oak some squirrel
    had once brought
        high into the air
clean leaves to: but

        reality can go to hell

is what the coon's eyes said to me:
and said how simple
the solution to my
problem is: it needs only
not to be: I thought the raccoon
felt no anger,
saw none; cared nothing for cowardice,
bravery; was in fact
bored at
knowing what would ensue:
the unwinding, the whirling growls,
exposed tenders,
the wet teeth—a problem to be
solved, the taut-coiled vigor
of the hunt
ready to snap loose:

you want to know what happened,
you want to hear me describe it,
to placate the hound's-mouth
slobbering in your own heart:
I will not tell you: actually the coon
possessing secret knowledge
pawed dust on the dogs
and they disappeared, yapping into
nothingness, and the coon went
down to the pond
and washed his face and hands and beheld
the world: maybe he didn't:
I am no slave that I
should entertain you, say what you want
to hear, let you wallow in
your silt: one two three four five:
one two three four five six seven eight nine ten:

            (all this time I've been
                counting spaces
while you were thinking of something else)
        mess in your own sloppy silt:
            the hounds disappeared
yelping (the way you would at extinction)
        into—the order
            breaks up here—immortality:
I know that's where you think the brave
        little victims should go:
            I do not care what
you think: I do not care what you think:
        I do not care what you
            think: one two three four five
six seven eight nine ten: here we go
        round the here-we-go-round, the
            here-we-go-round, the here-we-
go-round: coon will end in disorder at the
        teeth of hounds: the situation
            will get him:
spheres roll, cubes stay put: now there
        one two three four five
            are two philosophies:
here we go round the mouth-wet of hounds:

            what I choose
            is youse:
            baby

Unsaid

Have you listened for the things I have left out?
I am nowhere near the end yet and already
      hear
      the hum of omissions,
the chant of vacancies, din of

silences:

there is the other side of matter, antimatter,
      the antiproton:
      we
have measured the proton: it has mass: we
have measured the antiproton: it has negative mass:

you will not

hear me completely even at this early point
unless you hear my emptiness:
      go back:
      how can I
tell you what I have not said: you must look for it

yourself: that

side has weight, too, though words cannot bear it
out: listen for the things I have left out:
      I am
      aware
of them, as you must be, or you will miss

the nonsong

in my singing: it is not that words *cannot* say

what is missing: it is only that what is missing
            cannot
        be missed if
spoken: read the parables of my unmaking:

feel the ris-

ing bubble's trembling walls: rush into the domes
these wordy arches shape: hear
            me
        when I am
silent: gather the boundaried vacancies.

Raft

I called the wind and it
went over with me
   to the bluff
     that keeps the sea-bay
and we stayed around for a while
trying to think
    what to do:

I took some time to watch
the tall reeds
and bend their tassels
   over to my touch
     and
as the lowering bay-tide left
    salt-grass
combed flat toward the land
tried to remember
what I came to do:

in the seizures,
I could not think but
    vanished into the beauty
  of any thing I saw
and loved,
podstem, cone branch, rocking
    bay grass:

it was almost dark when the wind
breathless from playing
with water

came over and stopped
resting in the bare trees and dry grass
and weeds:

I built a fire in a hollow stump
and sitting by
wove a disc of reeds,
a round raft, and

sometime during the night
the moon shone but
it must have been the early night
for when I set out
standing on my disc
and poling with a birch
it was black dark
of a full tide:
the wind slept through my leaving:
I did not wake it to say goodbye:

the raft swirled before day
and the choppy, tugging bay
let me know
I had caught the tide
and was rushing through

the outer sea-banks
into the open sea:

when dawn came
I looked
and saw no land:

tide free and
without direction I
gave up the pole,
my round raft

having no bow,
nowhere to point:

I knelt in the center
to look for where the
    sun would break
and when it started to come
I knew the slow whirl
of my ship
which turned my back to the east
   and
brought me slowly round again:

at each revolution
    I had
new glory in my eyes
and thought with chuckles
   where would I be at noon
and what of the night
when the black ocean
might seem not there

though of course stars
    and planets rise and
east can be known
   on a fair night
but I was not
certain
I wanted to go east:
it seemed wise
   to let
the currents be
whatever they would be,
allowing possibility
to chance

where choice
   could not impose itself:

I knelt turning that way
    a long time,
glad I had brought my great
    round hat
for the sun got hot:

at noon
I could not tell
I turned
for overhead the sun,
    motionless in its dome,
spun still
and did not wobble
the dome
or turn a falling shadow
   on my raft's periphery:

soon though that symmetry
eased
    and the sun
was falling
and the wind came
   in an afternoon way

rushing before dark to catch me.

River

I shall
   go down
      to the deep river, to the moonwaters,
where the silver
willows are and the bay blossoms,

to the songs
   of dark birds,
      to the great wooded silence
of flowing
forever down the dark river

silvered at the moon-singing of hidden birds:

27 March

the forsythia is out,
   sprawling like
yellow amoebae, the long
      uneven branches—pseudo-
podia—
   angling on the bottom
of air's spring-clear pool:

shall I
   go down
      to the deep river, to the moonwaters,
where the silver
willows are and the bay blossoms,

to the songs

of dark birds,
to the great wooded silence
of flowing
forever down the dark river

silvered at the moon-singing of hidden birds.

Lines

Lines flying in, out: logarithmic
       curves coiling
toward an infinitely inward center: lines
     weaving in, threads lost in clustral scrawl,
        weaving out into loose ends,
wandering beyond the border of gray background,
     going out of vision,
        not returning;
or, returning, breaking across the boundary
     as new lines, discontinuous,
       come into sight:
fiddleheads of ferns, croziers of violins,
     convoluted spherical masses, breaking through
       ditchbanks where briar
stem-dull will
     leave and bloom:
       haunch line, sickle-like, turning down, bulging, nuzzling
under, closing into
     the hidden, sweet, dark meeting of lips:
       the spiraling out
or in
     of galaxies:
       the free-running wavy line, swirling
configuration, halting into a knot
     of curve and density: the broken,
       irreparable filament: tree-winding vines, branching
falling off or back, free,
     the adventitious preparation for possibility, from

branch to branch, ash to gum:
the breaker
    hurling into reach for shape, crashing
        out of order, the inner hollow sizzling flat:
the longnecked, uteral gourd, bass line
    continuous in curve,
        melodic line filling and thinning:
concentrations,
    whirling masses,
        thin leaders, disordered ends and risks:
explosions of clusters, expansions from the
    full radial sphere, return's longest chance:
        lines exploring, intersecting, paralleling, twisting,
noding: deranging, clustering.

The Strait

At the oracle
I found the
    god
though active
recalcitrant

unliteral as air:
the priestess
    writhed
and moaned
caught

in the anguish
of some
    perishable
event:
birds flew by:

the urns
hummed: the
    columns
glazed with
sun; on the

inside lit wet with
fire: another, not
    capable
of the inner
speech,

read the priestess

and said,
 "The
god wants honor,
desires in you

honor's attitude:
honor him and
 your
venture will
go well":

cannot, I said,
the god be
 more
specific? will
I honor

him? come again
safe to this
 grove?
the reader said,
"The

descent of the
god is
 awkward,
narrowing and
difficult; first

he is
loose in the
 air,
then captured,
held, by

holy fire: the

circle of columns
    binds
him and from
the columns

the priestess
gathers him,
    seized
by her struggling
mouth into

a speech of
forms: it is
    speech
few can read,
the god

violent to
overreach the
    definite:
why should
he, who is

all, commit
himself to the
    particular?
say himself
into less

than all? pressed
too far, he
    leaves
wounds that are
invisible: it

is only as
she becomes

him
that the priestess
cannot be hurt

or can be hurt:
should she
      break
her human hold
and go too far

with him,
who could bring
      her
back, her eyes
lost to the

visible? step
by step into the
      actual,
truth descending
breaks,

reaches us as
fragmentation
      hardened
into words":
but, I said, isn't

it convenient
the priestess is
      general
and inexact, merely
turning and wailing?

if the god fails
me, whom shall I
      blame?

her? you who may
have read her wrong?

and if all goes
well, whom shall I
    thank?
the god
with honor,

you with the
actual coin?
    "Night
falls," the reader said,
"the priestess lies

god-torn, limp: the
freed god
    flies
again blameless as
air: go

to your fate:
if you succeed, praise the
    god:
if you fail,
discover your flaw."

Identity

    1)   An individual spider web
          identifies a species:

an order of instinct prevails
        through all accidents of circumstance,
              though possibility is
high along the peripheries of
spider

                    webs:
                    you can go all
              around the fringing attachments

              and find
disorder ripe,
entropy rich, high levels of random,
        numerous occasions of accident:

    2)   the possible settings
          of a web are infinite:

    how does
the spider keep
          identity
    while creating the web
    in a particular place?

    how and to what extent
          and by what modes of chemistry
          and control?

it is
wonderful

how things work: I will tell you
              about it
              because

it is interesting
and because whatever is
moves in weeds
        and stars and spider webs
and known
                  is loved:
              in that love,
              each of us knowing it,
              I love you,

for it moves within and beyond us,
              sizzles in
winter grasses, darts and hangs with bumblebees
by summer windowsills:

              I will show you
the underlying that takes no image to itself,
              cannot be shown or said,
but weaves in and out of moons and bladderweeds,
              is all and
        beyond destruction
        because created fully in no
particular form:

              if the web were perfectly pre-set,
              the spider could
        never find
        a perfect place to set it in: and

              if the web were
perfectly adaptable,
if freedom and possibility were without limit,

                    the web would
lose its special identity:

          the row-strung garden web
keeps order at the center
where space is freest (interesting that the freest
               "medium" should
               accept the firmest order)

and that
order
                    diminishes toward the
periphery
          allowing at the points of contact
               entropy equal to entropy.

What This Mode of Motion Said

You will someday
try to prove me wrong
(I am the wings when you me fly)
to replace me with some mode
you made
and think is right:

I am the way by
which you prove me
wrong,
the reason you
reason against me:

I change shape,
turn easily into the shapes you make
and even you
in moving
I leave, betray:
what has not yet been imagined has been
imagined by me
whom you honor, reach for—
change unending though
slowed into nearly limited modes:

question me and I
will give you an answer

narrow and definite
as the question

that devours you (the exact

is a conquest of time that time vanquishes)
     or vague as wonder
by which I elude you:

          pressed
          for certainty
I harden to a stone,
lie unimaginable in meaning
     at your feet,

          leave you less
certainty than you brought, leave
     you to create the stone
as any image of yourself,
shape of your dreams:

     pressed too far
I wound, returning endless
inquiry
for the pride of inquiry:

          shapeless, unspendable,
          powerless in the actual
          which I rule, I

     will not
make deposits in your bank account
or free you from bosses
     in little factories,
will not spare you insult, will not
protect you from
men who
     have never heard of modes, who
do not respect me
or your knowledge of me in you;

men I let win,
their thin tight lips
humiliating my worshipers:

I betray
him who gets me in his eyes and sees
beyond the fact
to the motions of my permanence.

Nucleus

How you buy a factory:
    got wind of one for sale in

Montreal,
        Hochelaga
          where Cartier, amicably received,
      gave the squaws and children

tin bells and tin paternosters
and the men knives
        and went up to the nearby
height and
      called it Mt. Royal
from which the view was
panoramic,
      an island 17 × 40
miles,
        good trees (good as France)
        and, below, thick maize:

Montreal,
      got "The Laurentian" out of New York
first morning after the strike ended
and rode up parlor car (expense account)
        along the solid-white Hudson
        and on up into hilled
graybirch country, through the Adirondacks
and along the high west bank of Lake Champlain
        (on heavy ice

men in windhuts fishing)

and read Bottom
and gives to airy nothing
 a local habitation and a name:

  met the vice president
in the lobby at 8 next morning, ascended
(étage de confrères, troisième étage, s'il vous plaît,
  third floor, please)
to the 22nd floor
  to "The Panorama"
for breakfast: sight to see: St. Lawrence over there,
Windsor Hotel remodeling, where the Queen stayed,
  cathedral, replica (but smaller)
   of St. Peter's:

Montreal,
and left center city by cab,
  through the French Quarter, out near Westmont,
long stairs from street to second floor,
  said it was typical,
with metal viny rails,

  and on through streets, bilingual
traffic signs, turn left, left again: there:
Linden Street: 807, a local habitation and a name,

four walls, a limited, defined, exact place,
  a nucleus,
solidification from possibility:

  how you buy a factory:
determine the lines of
force
leading in and out, origins, destinations of lines;
determine how

[108]

from the nexus of crossed and bundled lines
the profit is
obtained, the
forces realized, the cheap made dear,
and whether the incoming or outgoing forces are stronger
and exactly why,
and what is to be done:

raw material inventory is
in winter
high: river frozen, must make half-year provisions,
squirrel-like, last till thaw, is
a warehousing problem: comes from England,
Germany (West):
important to keep a ready
stock of finished goods—customers won't wait, will
order from parent companies in England, Germany:
property taxes: things are
changing, you may get a rail siding here soon:
profit and loss sheet, cash flow, receivables:
large lot, vacancy providing for the future:
good machineshop and
here are the production lines:
how many heads on those machines: pcs per hr:
wages, skilled
unskilled: cut-off machines, annealing ovens, formers:
"I'll say! 15 below this morning."

order backlog: "I would say we have
an edge,
growth possibility: 50 good customers, pharma-
ceutical houses: you have to understand the background."
Perspective.

"Eight years ago . . . finally, I had to go to

Ottawa . . . left good man here, Oh, yes, he's done
fine . . . Swiss, later in Johannesburg;
        you understand, management
                wouldn't consider
selling him out, too much of himself": un-

favorable points: competition, international market,
low tariffs,
unprotected, only advantage personalized service
        to local
accounts, could
                buy elsewhere,
large firms in States have bigger machines, faster,
more production per hour

(more overhead, too)

"being small's our advantage . . . can adapt, work with
short runs of specialties—customers want
        their own designs, premium,
made-to-order prices. . . ."

Montreal,
        "sure to see McGill U., ice sculpture front of
each dorm, emblem"
cornless lawns,
            Cartier going through the motions of worship,
Indians looking up at sky, too,
can't see what:

"We'll get that information to you"
        further study
and in the deep cold night boarding train, bedroom
Yassuh,
and heat connections broken, cold, next morning
        going uptrain for toast and coffee,

that's where East River turns—Manhattan:
lines of force, winding, unwinding,
    nexus coiling in the mind:
        balance, judge: act.

Jungle Knot

One morning Beebe
　　　found on a bank of the Amazon
an owl and snake
　　　　dead in a coiled embrace:

　　　the vine prints its coil too deep into the tree
and leaved fire shoots greens of tender flame
　　　　rising among the branches,
drawing behind a hardening, wooden clasp:

the tree does not
　　　generally escape
though it may live thralled for years,
　　　succumbing finally rather than at once,

　　　in the vine's victory
the casting of its eventual death,
　　　though it may live years
on the skeletal trunk,

termites rising, the rain softening,
　　　a limb in storm
falling, the vine air-free at last, structureless as death:
　　　the owl,

　　　Beebe says, underestimated
the anaconda's size: hunger had deformed
　　　sight or caution, or
anaconda, come out in moonlight on the river bank,

had left half his length in shade: (you
　　　sometimes tackle

[112]

more than just what the light shows):
   the owl struck talons

      back of the anaconda's head
but weight grounded him in surprise: the anaconda
      coiled, embracing heaving wings
and cry, and the talons, squeezed in, sank

killing snake and owl in tightened pain:
   errors of vision, errors of self-defense!
errors of wisdom, errors of desire!
   the vulture dives, unlocks four eyes.

The Misfit

The unassimilable fact leads us on:
round the edges
      where broken shapes make poor masonry
the synthesis
fails (and succeeds) into limitation
      or extending itself too far
becomes a different synthesis:
law applies
      consistently to the molecule,
not to the ocean, unoriented, unprocessed,
it floats in, that floats in it:
      we are led on

to the boundaries
where relations loosen into chaos
      or where the nucleus fails to control,
fragments in odd shapes
expressing more and more the interstitial sea:
      we are led on

to peripheries, to the raw blocks of material,
where mortar and trowel can convert
      diversity into enlarging unity:
not the million oriented facts
but the one or two facts,
      out of place,

recalcitrant, the one observed fact
that tears us into questioning:
      what has not

joined dies into order to redeem, with
loss of singleness extends the form,
    or, unassimilable, leads us on.

Nelly Myers

I think of her
        while having a bowl of wheatflakes
(why? we never had wheatflakes
or any cereal then
except breakfast grits)
           and tears come to my eyes
and I think that I will die
because

        the bright, clear days when she was with me
and when we were together
(without caring that we were together)

can never be restored:
        my love wide-ranging
    I mused with clucking hens
and brought in from summer storms
at midnight the thrilled cold chicks
        and dried them out
        at the fireplace
and got up before morning
unbundled them from the piles of rags and
    turned them into the sun:

        I cannot go back
        I cannot be with her again

        and my love included the bronze
sheaves of broomstraw
she would be coming across the fields with

before the household was more than stirring out to pee

and there she would be coming
          as mysteriously from a new world
and she was already old when I was born but I love
the thought of her hand
wringing the tall tuft of dried grass

                    and I cannot see her beat out the fuzzy bloom
again
readying the straw for our brooms at home,
I can never see again the calm sentence of her mind
          as she
measured out brooms for the neighbors and charged
a nickel a broom:

I think of her
          but cannot remember how I thought of her
as I grew up: she was not a member of the family:
I knew she was not my mother
                    not an aunt, there was nothing
visiting about her: she had her room,
          she kept her bag of money
(on lonely Saturday afternoons
          you could sometimes hear the coins
spilling and spilling into her apron):
          she never went away, she was Nelly Myers, we
          called her Nel,
small, thin, her legs wrapped from knees to ankles
in homespun bandages: she always had the soreleg
                    and sometimes
red would show at the knee, or the ankle would swell
and look hot
          (and sometimes the cloths would
dwindle,

the bandages grow thin, the bowed legs look
pale and dry—I would feel good then,
         maybe for weeks
                  there would seem reason of promise,
      though she rarely mentioned her legs
and was rarely asked about them): she always went,

legs red or white, went, went
through the mornings before sunrise
                  covering the fields and
woods
looking for huckleberries
or quieting some wild call to move and go
         roaming the woods and acres of daybreak
and there was always a fire in the stove
when my mother rose (which was not late):

      my grandmother, they say, took her in
when she was a stripling run away from home
(her mind was not perfect
         which is no bar to this love song
                  for her smile was sweet,
      her outrage honest and violent)
and they say that after she worked all day her relatives
would throw a handful of dried peas into her lap
                  for her supper
and she came to live in the house I was born in the
northwest room of:

oh I will not end my grief
         that she is gone, I will not end my singing;
my songs like blueberries
felt-out and black to her searching fingers before light
welcome her
wherever her thoughts ride with mine, now or in any time

that may come
when I am gone; I will not end visions of her naked feet
in the sandpaths: I will hear her words
        "Applecandy" which meant Christmas,
"Lambesdamn" which meant Goddamn (she was forthright
            and didn't go to church
        and nobody wondered if she should

and I agree with her the Holcomb pinegrove bordering our
field was
more hushed and lovelier than cathedrals
        not to mention country churches with unpainted boards
and so much innocence as she carried in her face
has entered few churches in one person)

and her exclamation "Founshy-day!" I know no meaning
for but knew she was using it right:

and I will not forget how though nearly deaf
she heard the tender blood in lips of children
and knew the hurt
        and knew what to do:

and I will not forget how I saw her last, tied in a chair
lest she rise to go
and fall
            for how innocently indomitable
        was her lust
and how her legs were turgid with still blood as she sat
and how real her tears were as I left
        to go back to college (damn all colleges):
        oh where her partial soul, as others thought,
roams roams my love
mother, not my mother, grandmother, not my grandmother,
slave to our farm's work, no slave I would not stoop to:
I will not end my grief, earth will not end my grief,

I move on, we move on, some scraps of us together,
　　　my broken soul leaning toward her to be touched,
listening to be healed.

Motion for Motion

Watched on the sandy, stony bottom of the stream
the oval black shadow of the waterbeetle, shadow

larger than beetle, though no blacker, mirroring
at a down and off angle motion for motion, whirl, run:

(if you knew the diameters
of oval and beetle, the
depth of the steam, several
    indices of refraction
    and so forth

you might say why
the shadow outsizes the
beetle —

I admit to mystery
in the obvious —

but now that I remember some
I think the shadow
included the bent water where
the beetle rode, surface

tension, not breaking, bending
under to hold him up,

the deformation recorded in shade:
for light, arising from so far away,

is parallel
through a foot of water

(though edge-light
would

make a difference—a beetle can
exist among such differences
and do well):

someone has a clear vision of it all,
exact to complete existence;
loves me when I swear and praise
and smiles, probably, to see me
wrestle with sight

and gain no reason from it, or money,
but a blurred mind overexposed):

caught the sudden gust of a catbird, selfshot
under the bridge and out into my sight: he splashed
into the air near a briervine, lit:

I don't know by what will: it was clear sailing
on down the stream
and prettier—a moss-bright island made two streams
and then made one and, farther, two fine birches
and a lot of things to see: but he stopped

back to me,
didn't see me, hopped on through the vines, by some
will not including me . . .

and then there were two beetles, and later three at
once swimming in the sun, and three shadows,
all reproduced, multiplied without effort
or sound, the unique beetle—and I—lost to an

automatic machinery in things, duplicating, without
useful difference, some changeless order extending

[122]

backward beyond the origin of earth,

changeless and true, even before the water fell, or
the sun broke, or the beetle turned, or the still
human head bent from a bridge-rail above to have a look.

Visit

It is not far to my place:
you can come smallboat,
pausing under shade in the eddies
　or going ashore
　　to rest, regard the leaves

　or talk with birds and
shore weeds: hire a full-grown man not
late in years to oar you
　and choose a canoe-like thin ship;
　　(a dumb man is better and no

　costlier; he will attract
the reflections and silences under leaves:)
travel light: a single book, some twine:
　the river is muscled at rapids with trout
　　and a laurel limb

　will make a suitable spit: if you
leave in the forenoon, you will arrive
with plenty of light
　the afternoon of the third day: I will
　　come down to the landing

　(tell your man to look for it,
the dumb have clear sight and are free of
visions) to greet you with some made
　wine and a special verse:
　　or you can come by shore:

choose the right: there the rocks
cascade less frequently, the grade more gradual:
treat yourself gently: the ascent thins both
    mind and blood and you must
        keep still a dense reserve

    of silence we can poise against
conversation: there is little news:
I found last month a root with shape and
    have heard a new sound among
        the insects: come.

Expressions of Sea Level

Peripherally the ocean
marks itself
      against the gauging land
it erodes and
builds:

it is hard to name
the changeless:
speech without words,
      silence renders it:
and mid-ocean,

sky sealed unbroken to sea,
      there is no way to know
the ocean's speech,
intervolved and markless,
breaking against

      no boulder-held fingerland:
broken, surf things are expressions:
the sea speaks far from its core,
far from its center relinquishes the
long-held roar:
of any mid-sea
speech, the yielding resistances
of wind and water, spray,
swells, whitecaps, moans,
      it is a dream the sea makes,

an inner problem, a self-deep
dark and private anguish

revealed in small,
by hints, to
keen watchers on the shore:

only with the staid land
is the level conversation really held:
only in the meeting of rock and
                sea is
hard relevance shattered into light:

upbeach the clam shell
            holds smooth dry sand,
remembrance of tide:
water can go at
least that high: in

            the night, if you stay
to watch, or
if you come tomorrow at the right time,
you can see the shell caught
again in wash, the

sand turbulence-changed,
new sand left smooth: if
the shell washes loose,
flops over,
            buries its rim in flux,

it will not be silence for
a shell that spoke: the
            half-buried back will
tell how the ocean dreamed
breakers against the land:

into the salt marshes the water comes fast with rising tide:
an inch of rise spreads by yards
            through tidal creeks, round fingerways of land:

the marsh grasses stem-logged
combine wind and water motions,
        slow from dry trembling
to heavier motions of wind translated through
cushioned stems; tide-held slant of grasses
        bent into the wind:

        is there a point of rest where
        the tide turns: is there one
        infinitely tiny higher touch
on the legs of egrets, the
skin of back, bay-eddy reeds:
        is there an instant when fullness is,
        without loss, complete: is there a
        statement perfect in its speech:

how do you know the moon
is moving: see the dry
casting of the beach worm
        dissolve at the
delicate rising touch:

that is the
        expression of sea level,
the talk of giants,
of ocean, moon, sun, of everything,
spoken in a dampened grain of sand.

Still

I said I will find what is lowly
    and put the roots of my identity
    down there:
each day I'll wake up
and find the lowly nearby,
    and handy focus and reminder,
a ready measure of my significance,
the voice by which I would be heard,
the wills, the kinds of selfishness
    I could
freely adopt as my own:

but though I have looked everywhere,
    I can find nothing
    to give myself to:
    everything is

magnificent with existence, is in
surfeit of glory:
nothing is diminished,
nothing has been diminished for me:

I said what is more lowly than the grass:
    ah, underneath,
    a ground-crust of dry-burnt moss:
    I looked at it closely
and said this can be my habitat: but
nestling in I
found
    below the brown exterior

green mechanisms beyond intellect
awaiting resurrection in rain: so I got up

and ran saying there is nothing lowly in the universe:
I found a beggar:
he had stumps for legs: nobody was paying
him any attention: everybody went on by:
        I nestled in and found his life:
there, love shook his body like a devastation:
I said
        though I have looked everywhere
        I can find nothing lowly
        in the universe:

I whirled through transfigurations up and down,
transfigurations of size and shape and place:
        at one sudden point came still,
        stood in wonder:
moss, beggar, weed, tick, pine, self, magnificent
        with being!

The Yucca Moth

The yucca clump
   is blooming,
tall sturdy spears
   spangling into bells of light,
green
   in the white blooms
faint as a memory of mint:

I raid
   a bloom,
spread the hung petals out,
   and, surprised he's not
a bloom-part, find
   a moth inside, the exact color,
the bloom his daylight port or cove:

though time comes
   and goes and troubles
are unlessened,
   the yucca is lifting temples
of bloom: from the night
   of our dark flights, can
we go in to heal, live
   out in white-green shade
the radiant, white, hanging day?

The Constant

When leaving the primrose, bayberry dunes, seaward
I discovered the universe this morning,
      I was in no
mood
for wonder,
      the naked mass of so much miracle
already beyond the vision
of my grasp:

along a rise of beach, a hundred feet from the surf,
a row of clam shells
      four to ten feet wide
      lay sinuous as far as sight:

in one shell—though in the abundance
      there were others like it—upturned,
four or five inches across the wing,
a lake
three to four inches long and two inches wide,
all dimensions rounded,
      indescribable in curve:

and on the lake a turning galaxy, a film of sand,
coordinated, nearly circular (no real perfections),
      an inch in diameter, turning:
turning:
counterclockwise, the wind hardly perceptible from
      11 o'clock
        with noon at sea:
        the galaxy rotating,

        but also,
at a distance from the shell lip,
revolving
round and round the shell:

        a gull's toe could spill the universe:
two more hours of sun could dry it up:
a higher wind could rock it out:

the tide will rise, engulf it, wash it loose:
utterly:

the terns, their
        young somewhere hidden in clumps of grass or weed,
were diving *sshik sshik* at me,
        then pealing upward for a new round and dive:

I have had too much of this inexhaustible miracle:
miracle, this massive, drab constant of experience.

Motion

The word is
not the thing:
is
a construction of,
a tag for,
the thing: the
word in
no way
resembles
the thing, except
as sound
resembles,
as in *whirr*,
sound:
the relation
between what this
as word
is
and what is
is tenuous: we
agree upon
this as the net to
cast on what
is: the finger
to
point with: the
method of
distinguishing,

defining, limiting:
poems
are fingers, methods,
nets,
not what is or
was:
but the music
in poems
is different,
points to nothing,
traps no
realities, takes
no game, but
by the motion of
its motion
resembles
what, moving, is—
the wind
underleaf white against
the tree.

Corsons Inlet

I went for a walk over the dunes again this morning
to the sea,
then turned right along
    the surf
          rounded a naked headland
          and returned

    along the inlet shore:

it was muggy sunny, the wind from the sea steady and high,
crisp in the running sand,
    some breakthroughs of sun
  but after a bit

continuous overcast:

the walk liberating, I was released from forms,
from the perpendiculars,
    straight lines, blocks, boxes, binds
of thought
into the hues, shadings, rises, flowing bends and blends
    of sight:

        I allow myself eddies of meaning:
yield to a direction of significance
running
like a stream through the geography of my work:
    you can find
in my sayings

        swerves of action
        like the inlet's cutting edge:

[136]

there are dunes of motion,
organizations of grass, white sandy paths of remembrance
in the overall wandering of mirroring mind:

but Overall is beyond me: is the sum of these events
I cannot draw, the ledger I cannot keep, the accounting
beyond the account:

in nature there are few sharp lines: there are areas of
primrose
        more or less dispersed;
disorderly orders of bayberry; between the rows
of dunes,
irregular swamps of reeds,
though not reeds alone, but grass, bayberry, yarrow, all . . .
predominantly reeds:

I have reached no conclusions, have erected no boundaries,
shutting out and shutting in, separating inside
        from outside: I have
        drawn no lines:
        as

manifold events of sand
change the dune's shape that will not be the same shape
tomorrow,

so I am willing to go along, to accept
the becoming
thought, to stake off no beginnings or ends, establish
        no walls:

by transitions the land falls from grassy dunes to creek
to undercreek: but there are no lines, though
        change in that transition is clear
        as any sharpness: but "sharpness" spread out,
allowed to occur over a wider range

than mental lines can keep:

the moon was full last night: today, low tide was low:
black shoals of mussels exposed to the risk
of air
and, earlier, of sun,
waved in and out with the waterline, waterline inexact,
caught always in the event of change:
    a young mottled gull stood free on the shoals
    and ate
to vomiting: another gull, squawking possession, cracked a crab,
picked out the entrails, swallowed the soft-shelled legs, a ruddy
turnstone running in to snatch leftover bits:

risk is full: every living thing in
siege: the demand is life, to keep life: the small
white blacklegged egret, how beautiful, quietly stalks and spears
    the shallows, darts to shore
        to stab—what? I couldn't
  see against the black mudflats—a frightened
  fiddler crab?

    the news to my left over the dunes and
reeds and bayberry clumps was
    fall: thousands of tree swallows
    gathering for flight:
    an order held
    in constant change: a congregation
rich with entropy: nevertheless, separable, noticeable
    as one event,
      not chaos: preparations for
flight from winter,
cheet, cheet, cheet, cheet, wings rifling the green clumps,
beaks
at the bayberries:

  [138]

a perception full of wind, flight, curve,
sound:
the possibility of rule as the sum of rulelessness:
the "field" of action
with moving, incalculable center;

in the smaller view, order tight with shape:
blue tiny flowers on a leafless weed: carapace of crab:
snail shell:
        pulsations of order
        in the bellies of minnows: orders swallowed,
broken down, transferred through membranes
to strengthen larger orders: but in the large view, no
lines or changeless shapes: the working in and out, together
        and against, of millions of events: this,
                so that I make
                no form of
                formlessness:

orders as summaries, as outcomes of actions override
or in some way result, not predictably (seeing me gain
the top of a dune,
the swallows
could take flight—some other fields of bayberry
        could enter fall
        berryless) and there is serenity:

        no arranged terror: no forcing of image, plan,
or thought:
no propaganda, no humbling of reality to precept:

terror pervades but is not arranged, all possibilities
of escape open: no route shut, except in
    the sudden loss of all routes:

        I see narrow orders, limited tightness, but will

[139]

not run to the easy victory:
       still around the looser, wider forces work:
       I will try
    to fasten into order enlarging grasps of disorder, widening
scope, but enjoying the freedom that
Scope eludes my grasp, that there is no finality of vision,
that I have perceived nothing completely,
       that tomorrow a new walk is a new walk.

Saliences

Consistencies rise
and ride
the mind down
hard routes
    walled
with no outlet and so
to open a variable geography,
    proliferate
possibility, here
is this dune fest
    releasing,
mind feeding out,
gathering clusters,
fields of order in disorder,
where choice
can make beginnings,
    turns,
    reversals,
where straight line
and air-hard thought
can meet
unarranged disorder,
    dissolve
before the one event that
creates present time
in the multi-variable
    scope:
a variable of wind
among the dunes,

making variables
of position and direction and sound
of every reed leaf
and bloom,
running streams of sand,
winding, rising, at a depression
falling out into deltas,
weathering shells with blast,
striking hiss into clumps of grass,
against bayberry leaves,
      lifting
the spider from footing to footing
hard across the dry even crust
toward the surf:
wind, a variable, soft wind, hard
steady wind, wind
shaped and kept in the
bent of trees,
the prevailing dipping seaward
of reeds,
the kept and erased sandcrab trails:
wind, the variable to the gull's flight,
how and where he drops the clam
and the way he heads in, running to loft:
wind, from the sea, high surf
and cool weather;
from the land, a lessened breakage
and the land's heat:
wind alone as a variable,
as a factor in millions of events,
leaves no two moments
on the dunes the same:
      keep
free to these events,

bend to these
changing weathers:
multiple as sand, events of sense
alter old dunes
of mind,
release new channels of flow,
free materials
to new forms:
wind alone as a variable
takes this neck of dunes
out of calculation's reach:
come out of the hard
routes and ruts,
pour over the walls
of previous assessments: turn to
the open,
the unexpected, to new saliences of feature.

*

The reassurance is
that through change
continuities sinuously work,
cause and effect
        without alarm,
gradual shadings out or in,
motions that full
        with time
do not surprise, no
abrupt leap or burst: possibility,
with meaningful development
of circumstance:

when I went back to the dunes today,
        saliences,

congruent to memory,
spread firmingly across my sight:
the narrow white path
rose and dropped over
grassy rises toward the sea:
sheets of reeds,
tasseling now near fall,
filled the hollows
with shapes of ponds or lakes:
bayberry, darker, made wandering
chains of clumps, sometimes pouring
into heads, like stopped water:
   much seemed
constant, to be looked
forward to, expected:
from the top of a dune rise,
look of ocean salience: in
   the hollow,
where a runlet
   makes in
at full tide and fills a bowl,
extravagance of pink periwinkle
along the grassy edge,
and a blue, bunchy weed, deep blue,
deep into the mind the dark blue
   constant:
minnows left high in the tide-deserted pocket,
   fiddler crabs
bringing up gray pellets of drying sand,
disappearing from air's faster events
at any close approach:
certain things and habits
   recognizable as
having lasted through the night:

though what change in
a day's doing!
desertions of swallows
        that yesterday
ravaged air, bush, reed, attention
in gatherings wide as this neck of dunes:
now, not a sound
or shadow, no trace of memory, no remnant
        explanation:
summations of permanence!
where not a single single thing endures,
the overall reassures,
deaths and flights,
shifts and sudden assaults claiming
limited orders,
the separate particles:
earth brings to grief
much in an hour that sang, leaped, swirled,
yet keeps a round
        quiet turning,
beyond loss or gain,
beyond concern for the separate reach.

Dunes

Taking root in windy sand
  is not an easy
way
to go about
  finding a place to stay.

A ditchbank or wood's edge
  has firmer ground.

In a loose world though
  something can be started—
a root touch water,
  a tip break sand—

Mounds from that can rise
  on held mounds,
a gesture of building, keeping,
  a trapping
into shape.

Firm ground is not available ground.

Moment

He turned and
stood

in the moment's
height,

exhilaration
sucking him up,

shuddering and
lifting

him
jaw and bone

and he said
what

destruction am I
blessed by?

Glass

The song
sparrow puts all his
saying
into one
repeated song:
what

variations, subtleties
he manages,
to encompass denser
meanings, I'm
too coarse
to catch: it's

one song, an overreach
from which
all possibilities,
like filaments,
depend:
killing,

nesting, dying,
sun or cloud,
figure up
and become
song—simple, hard:
removed.

Configurations

1

when November stripped
    the shrub,
        what stood
        out
in revealed space was
a nest
    hung
    in essential limbs

2

    how harmless truth
    is
    in cold weather
    to an empty nest

3

dry
leaves
in
the
bowl,
        like wings

4

    summer turned light

into darkness
and inside the shadeful
shrub
the secret
worked
itself into life:

icicles and waterpanes:
recognitions:

at the bottom, knowledges
and desertions

5

speech comes out,
a bleached form,
nestlike:

after the events of silence
the flying away
of silence
into speech—

6

the nest is held
off-earth
by sticks;

so, intelligence
stays
out of the ground

erect on a
brittle walk of bones:

otherwise

the sea,

　　empty of separations

7

leaves
like wings
in the Nov
　　ember nest:

wonder where the birds are now that were here:
wonder if the hawks missed them:
wonder if

　　　　dry wings
　　　　lie abandoned,
　　　bodiless
　　　this
　　　November:

　　leaves—　　　　out of so many
　　　　　　　　a nestful missed the ground

8

I am a bush
I am a nest
I am a bird
I am a wind
I am a negg

　　I is a bush, nest, bird, wind, negg
　　I is a leaf

if I fall what falls:
the leaves fell and the birds flew away and winter came and

9

when
I
am   bringing
singing   those   home
,   two   again
summer   birds
comes
back

10

so what if
lots of
            unfathomable stuff
            remains,
            inconceivable distances,

            closed and open infinities:
so what if
all that, if
            thunderstorms spill the eggs,
            loosen the nest, strew it across
            galaxies of grass and weeds:

who cares what remains when
only the interior
            immaterial
            configuration—

            shape—
            mattered, matters, immaterial, unremaining

11

there is some relationship between
proximity

[152]

to the earth and permanence:

    a shrub puts itself into and out of
    the earth at once,
earth and air united by a stem's
polar meshes of roots and branches:

        earth
        shrub
        nest
        leaf
        bird

the bird is somewhere south, unoriented
    to these roots:
the leaves
    though they may not have wandered so far
are random:

        earth
        shrub
        nest

goodbye, nest, if wind lifts you loose
goodbye, shrub, if ice breaks you down
goodbye,
goodbye

12

the shrub is nothing
    except part of my song:
the bird I never saw is part of my song and
    nothing else:

(the leaves are a great many little notes I lost
    when I was trying to make the song
    that became my silence)

13

the cockbird longs for the henbird
which longs for the nest
    which longs for the shrub which
longs for the earth
which longs for the sun which longs for

14

inside there the woodmeat is saying
        please, please
          let me put on my leaves
          let me let the sap go

but the zero bark is saying
        hush, hush
          the time is not right
          it's not the right time

the woodmeat is always right
but bark is knowing

Reflective

I found a
weed
that had a

mirror in it
and that
mirror

looked in at
a mirror
in

me that
had a
weed in it

Butterflyweed

The butterfly that
named the weed
drank there, Monarch,
scrolled, medallioned—
his wings lifted close
in pale underwing salute

occasionally would
with tense evenness
open down

hinged coffers
lawned against the sun:
anchored in
dream, I could hardly
fall when earth
dropped and looped away.

Contingency

Water from the sprinkler
collects
in street-edge gravel and

makes rocky pools: birds
materialize—puff, bathe
and drink: a green-black

grackle lopes, listing,
across the hot street, pecks
a starling, and drinks: a

robin rears misty with
exultation: twittering comes
in bunches of starts and

flights: shadows pour
across cement and lawn: a
turn of the faucet
dries every motion up.

Trap

White, flipping
butterfly,
paperweight,

flutters by and
over shrubs,
meets a binary

mate and they
spin, two orbits
of an

invisible center;
rise
over the roof

and caught on
currents
rise higher

than trees and
higher and up
out of sight,

swifter in
ascent than they
can fly or fall.

Halfway

This October
rain
comes after fall

summer and
drought
and is

a still rain:
it takes leaves
straight

down: the
birches stand
in

pools of them-
selves, the yellow
fallen

leaves reflecting
those on
the tree that
mirror the ground.

Landscape with Figures

When I go back of my head
    down the cervical well, roots
        branch
thinning, figuring
    into flesh
and flesh
glimmers with man-old fires
and ghosts
hollowing up into mind
    cry from ancient narrowing
        needle-like caves:

a depth of contact there you'd
    think would hold, the last
        nerve-hair
feeding direct from
    meat's indivisible stuff:
but what we ride on makes us ride
and rootless mind
in a thundering rove
establishes, disposes:
    rocks and clouds
        take their places:

or if place shifts by a sudden breaking
    in of stars
        and mind whirls
where to go
    then like a rabbit it
freezes in grass, order

as rock or star, to let whatever can, come,
pass, pass over: somewhere another human
figure moves or rests, concern
    for (or fear of) whom
       will start and keep us.

Dark Song

Sorrow how high it is
that no wall holds it
back: deep

it is that no dam undermines
it: wide that it
comes on as up a strand

multiple and relentless:
the young that are
beautiful must die; the

old, departing,
can confer
nothing.

World

Breakers at high tide shoot
spray over the jetty boulders
that collects in shallow chips, depressions,

evening the surface to run-off level:
of these possible worlds of held water,
most can't outlast the interim tideless

drought, so are clear, sterile, encased with
salt: one in particular, though, a hole,
providing depth with little surface,

keeps water through the hottest day:
a slime of green algae extends into that
tiny sea, and animals tiny enough to be in a

world there breed and dart and breathe and
die: so we are here in this plant-created oxygen,
drinking this sweet rain, consuming this green.

Portrait

Dry-leaf life
curls up on
lobe toes

and like a lost
or haunted crab
skitters

across the street,
fretting at
the wind,

or curled forward
tumbles down or
even up a

rise, gay and
light as a
spring catkin,

or boatlike strikes
a stream or, wet,
flattens

out stream-bottom
in windless
black: come,

wind, away from
water and let
song spring &

leap with this
paper-life's
lively show.

Winter Scene

There is now not a single
leaf on the cherry tree:

except when the jay
plummets in, lights, and,

in pure clarity, squalls:
then every branch

quivers and
breaks out in blue leaves.

Loss

When the sun
falls behind the sumac
thicket the
wild
yellow daisies
in diffuse evening shade
lose their
rigorous attention
and
half-wild with loss
turn
any way the wind does
and lift their
petals up
to float
off their stems
and go

Recovery

All afternoon
the tree shadows, accelerating,
lengthened
till
sunset
shot them black into infinity:
next morning
darkness
returned from the other
infinity and the
shadows caught ground
and through the morning, slowing,
hardened into noon.

Interference

A whirlwind in the fields
lifts sand
into its motions
to show, tight, small,
the way it walks
through a summer day:

better take time to watch
the sand-shadow mist—
since every
grain of sand
is being counted by the sun.

Peak

Everything begins at the tip-end, the dying-out,
        of mind:
the dazed eyes set and light
dissolves actual trees:

        the world beyond: tongueless,
unexampled
burns dimension out of shape,
opacity out of stone:

come: though the world ends and cannot
end,
        the apple falls sharp
to the heart starved with time.

Passage

How, through what tube, mechanism,
unreal pass, does
    the past get ahead of us
to become today?

the dead are total mysteries, now:
their radiances,
    unwaxed by flesh, are put out:
disintegrations

occur, the black kingdom separates, loses
way, waters rush,
    gravel pours—
faces loosen, turn, and move:

that fact, that edge to turn around!
senselessly, then,
    celebrant with obscure
causes, unimaginable means, trickles

of possibility, the cull beads
catch centers, round out,
    luminescence stirs,
circulates through dark's depths

and there—all lost still lost—
the wells primed, the springs free,
    tomorrow emerges and
falls back shaped into today: endlessly.

Kind

I can't understand it
  said the giant redwood
    I have attained height and distant view,
    am easy with time,

  and yet you search the
  wood's edge
for weeds
that find half-dark room in margins
    of stone
    and are
as everybody knows
  here and gone in a season

  O redwood I said in this matter
I may not be able to argue from reason
but preference sends me stooping
seeking
    the least,
    as finished as you
    and with a flower

Height

There was a hill once wanted
to become a mountain
    and
forces underground helped it
  lift itself
  into broad view
and noticeable height:

but the green hills around and even
some passable mountains,
    diminished by white,
wanted it down
so the mountain, alone, found
  grandeur taxing and
  turned and turned
to try to be concealed:

oh but after the rock is
massive and high . . . !
    how many centuries of rain and
ice, avalanche
and shedding shale
  before the dull mound
can yield to grass!

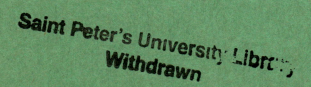